RHYTHMS of GRACE

FOREWORD by STOVALL WEEMS

KERRI WEEMS
CELEBRATION CHURCH

Published by Lifetogether Ministries,
Rancho Santa Margarita, CA

ISBN:
978-1-940077-21-5

Printed in the United States of America

CONTENTS

SESSIONS

APPENDICES

SMALL GROUP LEADERS

ENDORS

For the past year, I've been on a personal journey to remove busyness from my life. My friend, Kerri, provides us the perfect resource to turn down the clanging noise of chaos and set a life paced in rhythms of grace. With warmth, wisdom, and delightful teaching, this book is a treasure.

Lysa Terkeurst

NY TIMES BEST-SELLING AUTHOR OF UNGLUED AND PRESIDENT OF PROVERBS 31 MINISTRIES

I love and have great respect for Kerri Weems! Each visit with her leaves me sharpened and blessed. If you've ever felt overwhelmed, overworked, or overcome, Kerri Weems' important book Rhythms of Grace is just for you. With heartfelt maturity, Kerri beautifully reveals God's unlimited grace for every area of your life.

Amy Groeschel

CO-AUTHOR OF S.O.A.R. BIBLE STUDY FOR WOMEN

I'm so glad that my friend Kerri Weems wrote Rhythms of Grace. I believe it will help many women find their pace and hit their stride.

Lisa Bevere

MESSENGER INTERNATIONAL, BEST-SELLING AUTHOR/MINISTER, KISSED THE GIRLS AND MADE THEM CRY, FIGHT LIKE A GIRL, LIONESS ARISING

In a culture that tries to get us to live at a destructive pace, my friend Kerri Weems gives us some tools to navigate the big life we lead. In Rhythms of Grace, Kerri tells her own story of burn out and offers all of us real help in finding a healthy rhythm of life. This isn't a book that tells us to stop doing so much, or to slow down, rather it is a book that gives practical help on how to live the expansive life that God has called us to.

Holly Wagner

PASTOR OASIS CHURCH, FOUNDER GODCHICKS

If the pace of your life leaves you out of breath rather than energized, this book is for you. With practical insights, colorful stories, and a biblical foundation, Kerri motivates us to dive headlong into the craziness of life....at the pace God sets.

Tricia Lovejoy

SHARPENHER.COM, CONTRIBUTING WRITER, FLOURISH.ME, WIFE OF SHAWN LOVEJOY, PASTOR OF MOUNTAINLAKE.TV

EMENTS

This is a must read! We all long for a "grace-paced" life and in this book Kerri provides incredible wisdom and practical principles on how to discover and implement God's tempo for our lives.

Amy Bezet

LEAD PASTOR'S WIFE, BAYSIDE COMMUNITY CHURCH

This book is an amazing resource to "recalibrate" your life. I love how Kerri gives us tools for learning God's authentic rhythm personally created for each of us. Grace makes sense on a new level!

Caroline Barnett

CO-PASTOR OF ANGELUS TEMPLE AND THE DREAM CENTER

Every life has a rhythm to it. There are ups and downs, highs and lows, ins and outs. But too often, we try to set our own rhythm, forcing ourselves to live at a pace we were not created to keep. Too often we try to do all and be all. What we need to do is slow down and keep pace with the timing God has set for us. In Rhythms of Grace, my dear friend Kerri Weems reminds us in an uncompromising manner what it means to keep pace with God. Through personal reflection, humor, and authenticity, she opens her life to readers and draws us into her experiences. And with a gift that is undeniable, Kerri's insight and example remind us of what it means to live at the pace of grace in every situation in life!

Lisa Young

WIFE OF PASTOR ED YOUNG, FELLOWSHIP CHURCH, AUTHOR, THE CREATIVE MARRIAGE AND SEXPERIMENT, FOUNDER, FLAVOUR MINISTRY: WOMEN BECOMING WORLD CHANGERS

"Tired." "Worn out." "Burned out on religion." These are all outcomes we face if we don't allow Jesus to set the pace for our lives. Kerri Weems is a gifted wordsmith who tells it like it is, then brilliantly lifts our sights to a higher, unforced way of living. Rhythms of Grace is both powerful and practical, and a most recommended read for anyone wanting to live a significant life for Jesus.

Dianne Wilson

FOUNDING PASTOR OF NEWPORT CHURCH CALIFORNIA, BEST-SELLING AUTHOR & DIRECTOR OF THE IMAGINE FOUNDATION

As a mom of three and a pastor's wife, I know what it's like to feel overwhelmed and off-balance. The message of Kerri's book, Rhythms of Grace, brings our fast paced, perfection driven culture back to a Christ-centered pace of life. She gives great, practical tools to help us learn to enjoy every day and every season of life.

Holly Furtick

WIFE OF PASTOR STEVEN FURTICK, ELEVATION CHURCH

This book, Rhythms of Grace, is a life-giving, practical guide to finding and living in the grace tempo designed for each one of us individually. I know this is a book I need for my life and I believe will benefit the body of Christ. Kerri lives what she teaches in this book and wants everyone to benefit from all God has taught her, so we can find our rhythm of grace too! I love it!

Delynn Rizzo

ASSOCIATION OF RELATED CHURCHES

In our 30 plus years of friendship, I have always admired Kerri's consistent pursuit of growth, both personally and in her relationship with God. Rhythms of Grace shares beautifully simple, yet powerful principles on how to disconnect from the negative rhythms that may be influencing our pace in life and fall into step with God's divine rhythm for our lives.

Leslie Giebeling

THE LIFE CHURCH OF MEMPHIS

For all of us who have attempted to 'balance it all' and lost ourselves and who God created us to be in the process, Rhythms of Grace is a must-read. Kerri brilliantly intersects our lives with wisdom and practicality for both our spiritual journeys and our run-yourself-ragged daily lives. There are few books more important to our spiritual, mental and physical health as believers.

Lori Wilhite

AUTHOR OF LEADING AND LOVING IT, SENIOR PASTOR'S WIFE AT CENTRAL CHRISTIAN CHURCH IN LAS VEGAS

My gracious and beautiful friend, Kerri Weems, has an encouraging message in Rhythms of Grace for anyone who struggles with defining who they are through performance or accomplishments. Kerri's communication style is unique, clear, well-organized and easy to follow. With humility and honesty, she invites us into her inner world to demonstrate how the Lord has transformed her relationship with Him to be one of a continual, refreshing fellowship of rest. When we give the Lord freedom to create order and meaning on the inside, we have confidence to make choices that are in alignment with who He designed us to be all along. And the precious thing about Kerri is that this book describes exactly who she is – a woman of grace, willing by example to demonstrate how to walk in tempo with our gracious and loving Father God.

Michelle Bezet

WIFE OF PASTOR RICK BEZET, NEW LIFE CHURCH

ACKNOWLEDGMENTS

To Stovall, Kaylan, Stovie, and Annabelle. I couldn't have written the message of this curriculum without your love and support. There were lots of "mom-less" nights when I stayed up late to write in the study and mornings I slept in when you guys went to school. Thank you for your grace and being patient in the process.

To my mom, Karen, my dad Joe, and my sister, Darla. You all read through the manuscript and heard me talk about the message of this project ad nauseam until you probably couldn't stand it anymore. Thank you for believing in me and praying for me through the process.

To the Celebration Church staff and Celebration Sisterhood, thank you for being generous in releasing me to write and walk out the message of the book and curriculum. You have graciously allowed me to lead you and grow into the woman I am today.

To the friends who came alongside and helped me in the editorial and creative process: Chari Orozco, Linda Riddle, Lexie Goodman, Jenny Huang, John Phelps, Katelyn Barnes, the Celebration Creative team. Your insightful feedback and assistance with edits truly helped to shape this project.

To Brett Eastman and the Lifetogether team: thank you for your generosity and for believing in the message of *Rhythms of Grace*.

FOREWORD

Stovall Weems

I love a good beat. In fact, I just enjoy listening to different types of music in general. But there's something about the beat in a song that makes it unique. A good beat will move you. It can energize you. You might even start dancing to a rhythm without even realizing it!

If we think about the rhythm of our own lives, we might not describe it as something to dance to. For parents, the schedule is often rushed according to back-to-back school and extracurricular activities with the kids. For the college student, you might be cramming to study for class while also working full-time. For the businessman or young professional, you're meeting hectic deadlines or working around stressful co-workers, environments, and relationships.

On top of this, we live in an age where technology allows us to be accessible all the time. People can reach us 24/7. Many times, we're in a hurry to go somewhere, but we don't know why. We might always be thinking about the next thing to do, the next place to be, or the next person to talk to without being fully present in the here and now. It can be stressful just thinking about it!

That's why I'm so glad my wife, Kerri, wrote this small group curriculum to go along with her book, *Rhythms of Grace*. God has a perfect rhythm for each of our lives. This rhythm is not meant to be rushed or burdensome. It's a pace of grace that comes from the overflow of personal wholeness.

The message from this curriculum was born out of a season when Kerri and I were both experiencing stress and fatigue. As the Holy Spirit led us each in our own journeys of finding God's rhythm for our lives, I saw Kerri discover what true wholeness in Christ is meant to be and walk this out in her daily life.

Kerri is someone who truly lives from the inside-out. She leads with personal conviction, authenticity, and inner strength unlike anyone else. (Of course I might be biased because I married her!) What's interesting is that during the process of writing the *Rhythms of Grace* book and curriculum, Kerri actually took on greater responsibility as part of our Senior Executive Team in overseeing staff and leadership development as well as life development at our church. The scope of her responsibility in ministry increased, but Kerri stepped into it and found God's pace. I've seen her thrive in helping others develop their strengths and realize the full potential in Christ. She is still an incredible mom and wife. Kerri is walking out this journey of finding God's rhythm of grace and leading our staff and other ministry leaders to do the same.

We can read and talk about finding God's rhythm, but there is nothing more powerful than living it out with a group of friends. A community of relationships is where we can be sharpened, encouraged, and positioned to find true rest and peace in God. That's what the curriculum is all about. It is a tool to help you and a group of friends discover personal wholeness in Christ and equip you with the practical tools and principles to live this out daily. It's meant to be lived out together. Let's find God's beat for our lives and let this be what moves us.

STOVALL WEEMS | Lead Pastor, Celebration Church | Author, The God-First Life

WELCOME

Hello Friends!

Welcome to the Rhythms of Grace small group curriculum! Over the next six weeks your group will spend some time talking about what it means to live in wholeness, rest, and personal honesty - the foundational principles of my Rhythms of Grace book. My heart's desire is at the close of this study you will be ready to experience life at the peaceful, life-giving pace God has awaiting you.

Life in the 21st century is extremely fast-paced. A barrage of information and commitments are constantly competing for our time, attention, and energy. And in spite of the many ways technology makes our work easier, it has also made it possible for our work to invade every other aspect of our daily lives. As a result, it never seems like the work we have is finished. With the ability to accomplish more only a finger swipe away at all times, achievement and productivity have become the primary drivers of most of our lives instead of wholeness. This performance-based mindset leaves us feeling drained, empty, and ragged. Rhythms of Grace is God's message to a disjointed world that "stuff" will never make us whole, only Jesus can.

Through the next six sessions of this study, we will be discovering God's pace of grace. We will uncover the truths of shalom, Sabbath, and grace and understand how these profound spiritual principles relate to our everyday lives.

Along the way, you'll have a chance to learn together, to discuss and share your own stories in a way that focuses on practical, real-life application as you find rest in God's presence.

I believe that God is going to show up in your group because His desire for you is wholeness and peace. Are you ready and willing to hear from Him? I'm excited to see what God does in and through our time together. Let's get started!

In His Grace,

Kerri Weems

Kerri Weems

USING *this* WORKBOOK

Stuff to Help You Have a Great Small Group Experience

1 Notice in the Table of Contents there are three sections: (1) Sessions; (2) Appendix; and (3) Small Group Leaders. It will be helpful for you to get to know the Appendix sections. Some of them will be used in the sessions.

2 If you are leading or co-leading a small group, the section for Small Group Leaders will offer some hard-learned experiences of others that will encourage you and help you avoid many common obstacles to effective small group leadership. Make sure you take some time to read through the material – it will be a great help in your preparation.

3 Use this workbook as a guide, but put the needs of the group first. If you think of a better question than the next one in the lesson, ask it. If you sense that the members of your group want to spend some extra time in a particular section, do it. Don't measure success by how much material your group covers; Jesus did not say, "Go therefore and complete the curriculum." The goal is to have holy moments and to go deeper into community.

4 The best way to prepare for a great group experience is to pray. Pray for every group member and watch your heart for the group grow. Bring great expectation for God to show up in your group. Be specific in your prayers for what you are expecting God to do. If you aim for nothing, you'll hit it every time.

Now check out the Outline for Each Session on the following pages to understand how the sessions will flow.

OUTLINE of EACH SESSION

It can be easy for small groups to struggle with a very basic question: What do we do when we meet? That is why we have tried to provide more than enough content and questions for you. Inside this study guide you will find teaching, discussion, group exercises, and even some content for you to explore on your own during the week.

A typical group session for Rhythms of Grace will include the following:

WEEKLY MEMORY VERSE. For each session of Rhythms of Grace we have provided a memory verse emphasizing an important truth from the session. Memorizing Scripture is an important tool in the life transformation process (Romans 12:1-2). This is an optional exercise, but we encourage you to give this discipline a try. Ask the group if they want to try memorizing Scripture together. Give a few moments at the beginning of the group to allow group members to recite the verse they are memorizing.

SHARE YOUR STORY. A great definition of discipleship is, "You share your story. I share my story. Together we look at God's story in His Word, and gently, over time, our story becomes more like His story." As you can see from this definition, telling one's story is a key component of discipleship. Every person's story matters. So each week we provide an icebreaker to help group members tell a little of their story in a safe and fun way. Think of the icebreaker as a warm up. No athlete would ever compete in a game without warming up. Icebreakers help people warm up so that they can tell their story.

TEACHING. The Rhythms of Grace video teachings serve as an important companion to the Rhythms of Grace small group discussion book. This DVD contains brief teaching segments from Pastor Kerri Weems that accompany each week. Watching them with your group will prepare you for a time of meaningful discussion and growth.

DISCUSSION. During the discussion section, your group will begin to process the teaching you watched. We want your group to go beyond simply consuming the information presented and instead consider: "What is God saying to me? What is He saying to us as a group?" We want to help you apply the insights from Scripture practically and creatively, to your heart as well as your head.

APPLICATION. This section is about your group practically applying the lessons you are learning together. In the application section, we go beyond asking "What is God saying to me" to another, equally important question: "What am I going to do about it?" The Bible reminds us, "be doers of the Word, not just hearers" (James 1:22). We know that it is not simply enough to hear – we must take what we hear and make it a part of our everyday lives. This section will have a question or two that will challenge you to live out your faith in concrete and practical ways.

PRAYER. The group session will close with a time of prayer. Over the six weeks together, some may pray out loud for the very first time. The Prayer and Praise Report will help your group see and celebrate God's answers to prayer.

DAILY DEVOTIONS. The Daily Devotions provide short passages to read and reflect on your own between group meetings. This is a chance to slow down and read just a small portion of Scripture each day, and reflect and pray through it. They are not really "homework" assignments, but a chance to reflect further on what you learned in your group meeting. Use this section to seek God on your own throughout the week. This time at home should begin and end with prayer. Don't get in a hurry; take enough time to hear God's direction.

1

SESSION ONE

Unforced Rhythms of Grace

MEMORY Verse

"Come to Me, all you who are weary and burdened, and I will give you rest. Take My yoke upon you and learn from Me, for I am gentle and humble in heart, and you will find rest for your souls. For My yoke is easy and My burden is light." (Matthew 11:28-30 NIV).

Moving to the Beat of Heaven

Have you ever noticed that there is always more work to be done? Are the pressures and stresses of life shouting at you to move faster, accomplish more and perform better? Or maybe they make you want to quit...to just throw in the towel? Well, I have good news for you. God never intended for you to live in a hectic, chaotic way. In fact, He wants you to experience the unforced rhythms of His grace. He wants you to move to the song beat of Heaven.

Rhythms of Grace is all about tuning into the Holy Spirit and responding to what He says. He wants to set a life-giving, restful pace for your life.

SHARE your story

If your group is new, welcome newcomers. Introduce everyone—you may even want to have nametags for your first meeting.

Each of us has a story. The events of our life—good, bad, wonderful or challenging—have shaped who we are. God knows your story, and He intends to redeem it—to use every struggle and every joy to ultimately bring you to Himself. When we share our stories with others, we give them the opportunity to see God at work.

When we share our stories, we realize we are not alone—that we have common experiences and thoughts, and that others can understand what we are going through. Your story can encourage someone else, and telling it can be a path to freedom for you, and for those you share it with.

Open your group with prayer. This should be a brief, simple prayer, in which you invite God to be with you as you meet. You can pray for specific requests at the end of the meeting, or stop momentarily to pray if a particular situation comes up during your discussion.

As you begin, pass around a copy of the Small Group Roster on page 79 or a sheet of paper. Have everyone introduce themselves, then write down their contact information. Ask someone to make copies or type up a list with everyone's information and email it to the group during the week.

Then, use the following icebreaker question to get people talking.

Icebreaker:

What is your favorite kind of music? What music is currently on your playlist?

- ☐ Jazz
- ☐ Rhythm & Blues
- ☐ Rock n Roll
- ☐ Hymns
- ☐ Worship Music
- ☐ Other_______________

WATCH NOW:

DVD SESSION 1

Watch the DVD for this session now. Discuss the teaching you just experienced, as well as the Bible passage below.

DISCUSSION

If your group is new, welcome newcomers. Introduce everyone—you may even want to have nametags for your first meeting.

1. Read Matthew 11:28-30. What word or phrase jumps off the page to you and why?

   "Are you tired? Worn out? Burned out on religion? Come to me. Get away with me and you'll recover your life. I'll show you how to take a real rest. Walk with me and work with me—watch how I do it. Learn the unforced rhythms of grace. I won't lay anything heavy or ill-fitting on you. Keep company with me and you'll learn to live freely and lightly." The Message (MSG)

2. How would you describe your life right now?

   - ☐ Hamster running on a wheel
   - ☐ Throwing cargo over the side of a sinking ship
   - ☐ Silently suffering
   - ☐ Double life
   - ☐ Adrenaline junky
   - ☐ On cruise control
   - ☐ Other________________

3. What are some unhealthy ways that you deal with stress in your life?

   - ☐ Buy a calendar and start planning
   - ☐ Start cleaning
   - ☐ Go to sleep
   - ☐ Eat junk food
   - ☐ Watch television
   - ☐ Go buy something
   - ☐ Isolate
   - ☐ Other ________________

4. What kind of picture do the following verses paint of living one's life to the beat of heaven?
   John 10:10 John 16:27 Romans 14:17

5. Who is setting the rhythm of your life right now?

   - ☐ Boss
   - ☐ Kids
   - ☐ Spouse
   - ☐ Church
   - ☐ Other________________

APPLICATION

6. We've provided resources to help you with setting a healthy, grace pace in your life this week such as devotionals, and Scripture memory. Talk about what commitments you will make as a group this week to allow the song of heaven to set the pace of your life. Then, at your next meeting, talk about your progress and challenges.

7. Allow everyone to answer this question: "How can we pray for you this week?" Be sure to write prayer requests on your Prayer and Praise Report on page 86.

   Close the session in prayer.

notes

IMPORTANT GROUP LOGISTICS:

Whether your group is new or ongoing, it's always important to reflect on and review your values together. Take time right now to look at the Group Agreement on page 76. Read through it together and make sure everyone is on the same page about group expectations. An agreement assures that everyone clearly understands the values of the group and is committed to what will take your group to the next stage of intimacy and spiritual health.

We recommend that you rotate host homes on a regular basis and share the leadership of the meeting. We've come to realize that healthy groups invite the participation of all the group members. This helps to develop every member's ability to care for a few people in a safe environment. Even Jesus gave others the opportunity to serve alongside Him (Mark 6:30–44). Look at the FAQs in the Appendix for additional information about hosting or leading the group.

Use the Small Group Calendar on page 78 to plan who will host and lead each meeting. Take a few minutes to plan hosts and leaders for your remaining meetings. Don't pass this up! It will revolutionize your group by helping get everyone involved.

RHYTHMS

Unforced Rhythms of Grace

DAILY devotions

Day 1

READ ROMANS 12:2
"And do not be conformed to this world, but be transformed by the renewing of your mind, so that you may prove what the will of God is, that which is good and acceptable and perfect."

CONSIDER:
What do you think it means to renew your mind? Can you think of any verses you can meditate on that will transform your mind when it comes to experiencing God's rest and peace?

Day 2

READ MARK 4:19
"...but the worries of this life, the deceitfulness of wealth and the desires for other things come in and choke the word, making it unfruitful."

CONSIDER:
What worries or desires are keeping you from letting the rhythms of grace set the pace of your life? What heavy or ill-fitting yokes have you been carrying? What other things beside grace might be driving you?

Day 3

READ EPHESIANS 4:23-24
"...to be made new in the attitude of your minds; and to put on the new self, created to be like God in true righteousness and holiness."

CONSIDER:
What role do you believe rest can play in putting on your new self and partaking in God's character? What is the pace of your life like at this moment? Are there regular intervals of rest? How do you think incorporating regular rhythms of rest would impact your life?

Use these daily devotions to go deeper into this week's topic. Each day, read the verse given. Take your time. Ask God to speak to you through His Word. Listen to what He wants to say to you, and respond to Him as you meditate on the truths you find in each Scripture.

On the first day of the week, you may want to read through all of the verses given for the week so you can get the "big picture" of the passage. After that, walk slowly verse by verse. Listen to what God wants to say to you through His Word, and respond to Him as you meditate on the truths of Scripture.

Day 4

READ EPHESIANS 5:17
"Therefore do not be foolish, but understand what the Lord's will is."

CONSIDER:
What level of priority do you think that God puts on your rest and wholeness? What do you believe His will is regarding the pace of your life?

Day 5

READ COLOSSIANS 3:10
"...and have put on the new self, which is being renewed in knowledge in the image of its Creator."

CONSIDER:
How does God model rest for us in the Bible? What do you imagine the beat of Heaven's song to feel like?

Day 6

Use the following space to write any thoughts about what God has been speaking to you through this week's session and during your devotional time. You may also want to write down observations or questions that you'd like to share with the group at your next meeting.

2 SESSION TWO

Shalom

MEMORY Verse

"But He was wounded for our transgressions, He was bruised for our iniquities; upon Him was the chastisement that brought us peace, and with His stripes we are healed."(Isaiah 53:5 KJV)

God's "Box Top" for Your Life

Have you ever put together a giant puzzle with a thousand tiny pieces? If you have, then you know that it's nearly impossible to have any idea how the pieces are supposed to fit together unless you look at the image on the top of the puzzle box as a guide. Without that image on the box top, all those pieces are just too complicated to fit together in a way that makes sense! Life can sometimes be like a puzzle. There are many different "pieces" that need to fit together to give our lives shape and meaning. Marriage, work, church activities, family, and friends are just some of the pieces of our lives' puzzles that we need to fit together to form a complete picture of the life we hope for. Many times we are arranging the pieces of our lives with the wrong box top in view. But, did you know that God has a "box top" for what the good life looks like? His name is Jesus, the Prince of Peace. The Hebrew word for peace is *shalom* which is defined as wholeness.

Yes, God wants perfect wholeness in your life; soundness from top to bottom, nothing missing, nothing lost. Amidst the deceptive box tops of achievement, productivity, fame, fortune, and success, Jesus is the only one who can truly answer the question of your significance and value and He is the only one whose answer will leave you satisfied.

SHARE your story

When we share our stories, we can encourage someone else and learn.

We can experience the presence of God, as He helps us be brave enough to reveal our thoughts and feelings.

Open your group with prayer. This should be a brief, simple prayer, in which you invite God to guide you as you meet; to give you insight and wisdom. You can pray for specific requests at the end of the meeting or stop momentarily to pray if a particular situation comes up during your discussion.

Then, use the following icebreaker to get people talking.

Icebreaker:

How peaceful is your life right now on a scale of 1 to 10 with 10 being extremely peaceful! Use the 1 to 10 scale to describe how peaceful the following areas of your life are: friendships, family, marriage, work etc.

What is your definition of peace?

WATCH NOW:

DVD SESSION 2

Watch the DVD for this session now. Discuss the teaching you just experienced, as well as the Bible passage below.

ISERVE

DISCUSSION

1. What do you think of the strategy of ordering your external world and circumstances in order to find internal peace?

"Therefore, since we have been made right in God's sight by faith, we have peace with God because of what Jesus Christ our Lord has done for us. Because of our faith, Christ has brought us into this place of undeserved privilege where we now stand, and we confidently and joyfully look forward to sharing God's glory." Romans 5:1-2
New Living Translation (NLT)

2. Kerri defines the peace of God, shalom, as "Soundness from top to bottom, wholeness, nothing missing, nothing lost." How does this definition differ from your definition of peace when you began this study? How does this definition change how you pursue peace in your life?

3. Brokenness in our lives blocks us from experiencing wholeness. Kerri's brokenness was establishing her value and significance through achievement. What are some of the ways that we seek to answer the question of value and significance in our lives?

4. From the list created in question three, where are you most likely to look to establish your value and significance?

5. What are some of the pitfalls of defining your value through achievement and the lists you have created in question three?

6. Read Romans 5:1-2. How do we find the peace we are looking for according to this verse?

APPLICATION

7. Talk in your group about how you can find the wholeness you are looking for through a personal relationship with Jesus Christ.

Close your meeting with prayer. Don't forget to use the Prayer & Praise report in the Appendix.

notes

SHALOM

DAILY devotions

Day 1

READ ISAIAH 9:6

"For a child will be born to us, a son will be given to us; And the government will rest on His shoulders; and His name will be called Wonderful Counselor, Mighty God, Eternal Father, Prince of Peace."

CONSIDER:

What does it mean to you that Jesus is our Prince of Peace? Now that you know the biblical definition of peace (wholeness), is it different from the way you viewed peace previously?

Day 2

READ ISAIAH 26:3

"You will keep in perfect peace those whose minds are steadfast, because they trust in you."

CONSIDER:

Where do you take your question of value? Are you taking it to external things such as achievement, productivity, monetary success, popularity? Or to Jesus? Are you experiencing wholeness in your mind, soul, and body as a result?

Day 3

READ ISAIAH 26:12

"Lord, You establish peace for us; all that we have accomplished You have done for us."

CONSIDER:

We have been made in the image of God. We were originally created to be in complete wholeness, along with the rest of creation. When Adam and Eve turned away from God, everything after became broken and shattered. But Jesus came to restore wholeness and to once again rebuild the picture of God's box top. Have you let your craving for significance draw you to God? Do you realize that you don't have to do any type of work or performance for God to love you? As Isaiah 26:12 says, "all that we have accomplished You have done for us."

Use these daily devotions on your own between meetings. Each day, read the verse given. Take your time. Ask God to speak to you through His Word. Notice which words or phrase stands out to you. Then take some time to journal your response back to him. You can write whatever's on your heart. Answer the "consider" question only if it's helpful. Feel free to go another direction if you sense God leading you.

On the first day, you may want to read over all the verses for the week to get the "big picture" of the passage. But then walk slowly verse by verse. Listen to what God wants to say to you through His Word, and respond to Him as you meditate on the truths of Scripture.

Day 4

READ ISAIAH 54:10

"For the mountains shall depart and the hills be removed, but My kindness shall not depart from you nor shall My covenant of peace be removed," says the Lord who has mercy on you."

CONSIDER:

Are you comforted by the fact that everything else, including this earth, will pass away, but the salvation of the Lord will remain forever? Does this change the way you view what is important in your life?

Day 5

READ PSALM 4:7-8

"You have put gladness in my heart, More than when their grain and new wine abound. In peace I will both lie down and sleep, For you alone, O Lord, make me to dwell in safety."

CONSIDER:

In knowing that God's goal for your life is wholeness, not achievement, does it put gladness in your heart? Does it produce a feeling of relief? Does it allow the necessity of rest to become more important to you?

Day 6

Use the following space to write any thoughts about what God has been speaking to you through this week's session and during your devotional time. You may also want to write down observations or questions that you'd like to share with the group at your next meeting.

3 SESSION THREE

Sabbath - God's Baseline Beat

MEMORY Verse

"Then He said to them, 'The Sabbath was made for man, not man for the Sabbath.'" (Mark 2:27 NIV)

Free in Christ to Rest in His Grace

Rhythm is best summarized in two ways: consistent and repeatable. Just like your favorite song, rhythm has a beat that consistently repeats at regular intervals. Rhythm is extremely important when there are a lot of pieces layering together. For example, think of the importance of rhythm in the context of a symphony or orchestra. Similar to music, God has set a baseline beat, or rhythm, for our lives. In fact, that's why this book is called Rhythms of Grace. Sabbath was created by God to be a regularly recurring rhythm of rest renewal. The message that Sabbath speaks to us is loud and clear: "You are free." You are free from the tyranny of things that seem urgent; free from the "taskmasters" driving your life. God wants you to set apart time each week to experience His presence in a new and refreshing way. Sabbath, simply put, is a time dedicated to rest. Be free in Christ to rest in His grace.

SHARE your story

Open your group with prayer. This should be a brief, simple prayer in which you invite God to be with you as you meet.

You can pray for specific requests at the end of the meeting, or stop momentarily to pray if a particular situation comes up during your discussion.

Telling our personal stories builds deeper connections among group members. A great way to begin your group is by taking a few moments to talk about how everyone did applying the lesson from last week. Our goal for gathering is to live out the rhythms of grace in our everyday lives.

Begin your time together by using the icebreaker to get people talking.

Icebreaker:

What kind of dancer are you? Describe your rhythm.

- ☐ Fred Astaire
- ☐ I dance like Hitch from the movie Hitch
- ☐ I don't dance
- ☐ Other ________________

WATCH NOW:
DVD SESSION 3

Watch the DVD for this session now. Discuss the teaching you just experienced, as well as the Bible passage below.

DONT

DISCUSSION

1. What is God's baseline rhythm according to the following verses:

   Genesis 2:2 Exodus 20:8-10

2. When you think of Sabbath, what is the first thought that comes into your mind?

3. Give yourself a letter grade (A,B,C,D,F) on "doing nothing."

4. Read 2 Corinthians 3:17. What do you think of this statement that Kerri makes, "If you can't rest, if you won't rest, then are you truly free?"

   "Now the Lord is the Spirit, and where the Spirit of the Lord is, there is freedom." New International Version (NIV)

5. What are the taskmasters in your life that won't let you rest?

6. Study the life of Jesus in the following verses. What do we learn from Jesus about rest?

   Matthew 14:23 Mark 6:31-32 Luke 5:16

APPLICATION

7. A rhythm is that which repeats and is consistent. Talk as a group how you can establish a rhythm of rest that repeats and is consistent. Talk about the steps you will take to create a Sabbath Zone in your life.

Close your meeting with prayer. Don't forget to use the Prayer & Praise report in the appendix.

notes

SABBATH

Sabbath – God's Baseline Beat

DAILY devotions

Day 1

READ GENESIS 2:2-3

"By the seventh day God completed His work which He had done, and He rested on the seventh day from all His work which He had done. Then God blessed the seventh day and sanctified it, because in it He rested from all His work which God had created and made."

CONSIDER:

Why do you think it was so important for God to model rest for us? What are some things that keep you from experiencing a regular interval of rest?

Day 2

READ PSALM 62:1-2

"My soul finds rest in God alone; my salvation comes from Him. He alone is my rock and my salvation; He is my fortress, I will never be shaken."

CONSIDER:

In what ways can you create a "Sabbath Zone" in your life? Are you linking your value to anything other than Christ? If so, what are those things? How are those things enslaving you rather than freeing you?

Day 3

READ HEBREWS 4:9

"So there remains a Sabbath rest for the people of God."

CONSIDER:

Did you know that the Sabbath isn't just a Jewish idea? Did you know that it is God's idea, which He established at the creation of the world? How does this change your perspective on entering into this rest?

As you've done in prior weeks, use this section to stay connected with Jesus through your week on your own. Each day, read the verse given. Take your time. Ask God to speak to you through His Word. Notice which word or phrase stands out to you. Then take some time to journal your response back to him. You can write whatever's on your heart. Answer the "consider" question only if it's helpful. Feel free to go another direction, if you sense God leading you.

On the first day of the week, you may want to read through all of the verses given for the week so you can get the "big picture" of the passage. After that, walk slowly verse by verse. Listen to what God wants to say to you through His Word, and respond to Him as you meditate on the truths of Scripture.

Day 4

READ HEBREWS 4:10

"...for anyone who enters God's rest also rests from their works, just as God did from His."

CONSIDER:

What are some things that you love to do that allow you to rest from everyday work?

Day 5

READ MARK 6:31

"Then, because so many people were coming and going that they did not even have a chance to eat, He said to them, 'Come with me by yourselves to a quiet place and get some rest.'"

CONSIDER:

Do you ever feel as physically, mentally, and spiritually exhausted as Jesus' disciples felt in this verse? In those moments, do you realize that Jesus wants you to come away with Him and rest? How does this invitation of rest make you feel?

Day 6

Use the following space to write any thoughts about what God has been speaking to you through this week's session and during your devotional time. You may also want to write down observations or questions that you'd like to share with the group at your next meeting.

4

SESSION FOUR

Grace in Your Everyday Life

MEMORY Verse

"The Word became flesh and blood, and moved into the neighborhood. We saw the glory with our own eyes, the one-of-a-kind glory, like Father, like Son, Generous inside and out, true from start to finish." (John 1:14 MSG)

Laboring Under the Load of Perfection

Sometimes life can feel compartmentalized, right? We have our spiritual life, then our family life, our work life, our time with friends, and then after all of that we try to fit in exercise, fun hobbies, etc. Your life may be prioritized in a different order, but we all feel the pressure in one way or another. The majority of our lives take place in areas that most of us wouldn't describe as very spiritual. Too often we separate our lives into two halves: the spiritual (sacred) and then the secular. God wants us to realize that every aspect of our lives is important to Him. It is all worship to and for Him. He is not intimidated by our mess; so invite Him in! Invite Him in as you are cooking dinner for your family; invite Him in when you are sending emails to clients; invite Him in when you are studying for that midterm test. He wants to be with you in even these moments!

SHARE your story

Open your group with prayer. This should be a brief, simple prayer, in which you invite God to be with you as you meet.

You can pray for specific requests at the end of the meeting or stop momentarily to pray if a particular situation comes up during your discussion.

Telling our personal stories builds deeper connections among group members. A great way to help people tell their stories is by asking them to share a high or low since you last met together. A high is anything good that has happened in their life, and a low is anything hard that has happened in their life. If someone shares something extremely difficult or tragic make sure you stop and pray for them in the moment.

Begin your time together by using the following icebreaker to get people talking.

Icebreaker:

-What was your first job?
-What has been your favorite job?
-What job did you hate the most?

WATCH NOW:
DVD SESSION 4

Watch the DVD for this session now. Discuss the teaching you just experienced, as well as the Bible passage below.

DISCUSSION

1. When do you feel most spiritual, most connected to God?

2. Question one talks about connecting to God, how much of your everyday life do you spend doing what most connects you to God?

3. Agree or Disagree and Why?

God cares as much about the spreadsheet creation, the phone calls and the emails as He does prayer. It is all worship to Him.

4. How do the following two verses impact your view of connecting to God in your everyday life?

   "So whether you eat or drink or whatever you do, do it all for the glory of God."
   1 Corinthians 10:31 New International Version (NIV)

   Whatever you do, work at it with all your heart, as working for the Lord, not for human masters..."
   Colossians 3:23 New International Version (NIV)

5. In what areas of your life do you labor under the heavy burden of perfectionism and performance-based acceptance?

APPLICATION

6. Apply 2 Corinthians 12:9-10 to the areas of your life where you are imperfect and fall short of your own and others expectations.

"Because of the surpassing greatness of the revelations, for this reason, to keep me from exalting myself, there was given me a thorn in the flesh, a messenger of Satan to torment me—to keep me from exalting myself! Concerning this I implored the Lord three times that it might leave me. And He has said to me, "My grace is sufficient for you, for power is perfected in weakness." Most gladly, therefore, I will rather boast about my weaknesses, so that the power of Christ may dwell in me. Therefore I am well content with weaknesses, with insults, with distresses, with persecutions, with difficulties, for Christ's sake; for when I am weak, then I am strong." 2 Corinthians 12:7-10 New American Standard Bible (NASB)

Close your meeting with prayer. Don't forget to use the Prayer & Praise Report in the Appendix. Often when we pray for the needs of others we may find that God is prodding us to be a part of the answer to that prayer. One way we do this is by serving others. Groups grow closer when they serve together. How could you as a group serve someone in need? You may want to provide a meal for a family going through difficulty, or give some practical help to someone in need. If nothing comes to mind, spend some time as a group praying and asking God to show you who needs your help. Have two or three group members organize a serving project for the group, and then—do it!

There are two more sessions in this study. It's not too soon to think about whether your group will continue after you complete this study. Think and pray about it—you don't have to decide just yet.

notes

GRACE

Grace in Your Everyday Life

DAILY devotions

Day 1

READ 2 CORINTHIANS 12:9
"But He said to me, 'My grace is sufficient for you, for My power is made perfect in weakness.' Therefore I will boast all the more gladly of my weaknesses, so that the power of Christ may rest upon me."

CONSIDER:
What are some things in your life that you would consider weaknesses? How does it make you feel to know that Christ's power is made perfect in those very things? Are you striving and laboring under the weight of a perfectionist attitude? You were never meant to labor under the load of perfection. God's grace is sufficient for everything for everything you need and everything you are.

Day 2

READ PHILIPPIANS 4:13
"I can do all things through Christ who strengthens me."

CONSIDER:
Are there moments throughout the day that you pause and recognize God's presence? Are you giving God a space to fill in your everyday life? If not, what are some ways that you can begin doing this? If you struggle to remember God in your everyday routine, try fasting. You can also pray the Lord's Prayer throughout the day to keep your mind focused on Him.

Day 3

READ COLOSSIANS 3:17
"Whatever you do in word and deed, do in the name of the Lord Jesus, giving thanks through Him to God the Father."

CONSIDER:
In what way can you cultivate an attitude of thanksgiving throughout your day? Have you invited God into your work day, or other parts of your day that you would normally consider to be more "secular" areas of your life? If not, invite Him today and see how it changes your perspective on work for the better!

Use these daily devotions on your own between group meetings. Each day, read the verse given. Take your time. Ask God to speak to you through His Word. As you read, notice which word or phrase stands out to you. Then take some time to journal your response back to him. You can write whatever's on your heart. Answer the "consider" question only if it's helpful. Feel free to go another direction, if you sense God leading you.

On the first day of the week, you may want to read through all of the verses given for the week so you can get the "big picture" of the passage. After that, walk slowly verse by verse. Listen to what God wants to say to you through His Word, and respond to Him as you meditate on the truths of Scripture.

Day 4

READ ROMANS 12:1-2

"Therefore I urge you, brethren, by the mercies of God, to present your bodies a living and holy sacrifice, acceptable to God, which is your spiritual service of worship."

CONSIDER:

Have you ever thought of your work as worship? If not, why not start today? Think of one or two ways that you serve God in your work. Perhaps doing part of a project that nobody else wants to do, cleaning up someone else's microwave splatters, or speaking kindly of someone who has rejected or wronged you. The next time one of those situations arise, take a moment and offer it up to God as an act of worship. What other ways can you apply this concept to your current work situation?

Day 5

READ 1 CORINTHIANS 3:9

"For we are co-workers in God's service; you are God's field, God's building."

CONSIDER:

Have you ever considered that all of God's children are ministers and missionaries; not just the ones who work in a physical church building? How can God co-labor with you where you are right now? How can you co-labor with God?

Day 6

Use the following space to write any thoughts about what God has been speaking to you through this week's session and during your devotional time. You may also want to write down observations or questions that you'd like to share with the group at your next meeting.

5 SESSION FIVE

How to Live with Intentionality

MEMORY Verse

"Therefore, since we have so great a cloud of witnesses surrounding us, let us also lay aside every encumbrance and the sin which so easily entangles us, and let us run with endurance the race that is set before us, fixing our eyes on Jesus, the author and perfecter of faith, who for the joy set before Him endured the cross, despising the shame, and has sat down at the right hand of the throne of God." (Hebrews 12:1 NASB)

Living with Intentionality

Time is a precious asset. It is precious because we can't make more of it nor can we slow it down. That leaves us one option: to sanctify it. To sanctify something means to set it apart; to see it as something sacred. Time that is sanctified is time that is set apart for the use of God. The Memory Verse from this week is from Hebrews 12 and says, "...let us run with endurance the race that is set before us, fixing our eyes on Jesus, the author and perfecter of faith..." God is telling us to run our race with endurance. He wants us to be in this for the long haul. That certainly doesn't mean He wants you limping, crawling, and dragging yourself disheveled and bandaged across the finish line. He wants you to finish strong with wholeness. What does wholeness look like for you in this very season of your life?

SHARE *your story*

Open your group with prayer. This should be a brief, simple prayer in which you invite God to be with you as you meet.

You can pray for specific requests at the end of the meeting, or stop momentarily to pray if a particular situation comes up during your discussion.

Telling our personal stories builds deeper connections among group members. Sharing our stories requires us to be honest. We can help one another to be honest and open by creating a safe place: be sure that your group is one where confidentiality is respected, where there's no such thing as "stupid questions," where you listen without criticizing one another.

To help people share their personal story ask them, "On a scale of 1 to 10 with 1 being horrible and 10 being awesome, how was day today?" When they give their number, ask them to explain how they came up with that number.

Begin your time together by using the following icebreaker to get people talking.

Icebreaker:

Which one of these phrases describes you best in most situations?

☐ Make it up as you go; likes options

☐ Intentional, structured; planned

WATCH NOW:

DVD SESSION 5

Watch the DVD for this session now. Discuss the teaching you just experienced, as well as the Bible passage below.

DISCUSSION

1. When it comes to controlling your schedule, how are you doing?

☐ Out of control
☐ Inconsistent
☐ Under Control
☐ Other ____________________

2. What do the following verses teach us about time?

"Redeeming the time, because the days are evil."
Ephesians 5:16 King James Version (KJV)

"Look here, you people who say, "Today or tomorrow we are going to such and such a town, stay there a year, and open up a profitable business." How do you know what is going to happen tomorrow? For the length of your lives is as uncertain as the morning fog—now you see it; soon it is gone." James 4:13-14 Living Bible (TLB)

3. How much margin do you have built in your life?

☐ None
☐ I live in deficit
☐ A little
☐ A lot
☐ Other ____________________

4. Which one of these principles of intentionality is most helpful to you?

☐ Saying yes to something whether you realize it or not means you have automatically said no to something else.

☐ Decide beforehand the limits of what you will do. For example, decide to do only one major event on the weekend.

☐ A schedule that is 70% full is full. Plan margin into your schedule.

APPLICATION

5. Read Hebrews 12:1. Notice how Hebrews 12:1 speaks about intentionality in winning the race. How will you be more intentional with the limited time that you have so that you are able to endure, to finish the race well?

"Therefore, since we have so great a cloud of witnesses surrounding us, let us also lay aside every encumbrance and the sin which so easily entangles us, and let us run with endurance the race that is set before us." Hebrews 12:1 New American Standard Bible (NASB)

Close your meeting with prayer. Don't forget to use the Prayer & Praise Report in the Appendix.

notes

LIVE

How to Live with Intentionality

DAILY devotions

Day 1

READ EPHESIANS 5:15-17

"Look carefully then how you walk, not as unwise but as wise, making the best use of time, because the days are evil. Therefore do not be foolish, but understand what the will of the Lord is."

CONSIDER:

Do you set aside time in your weekly schedule to prioritize the things that are really important to you – things that you know will matter in the long run? Are you planning for margin in your schedule?

Day 2

READ MATTHEW 6:33

"But seek first the kingdom of God and His righteousness, and all these things will be added to you."

CONSIDER:

What are you seeking first? Is seeking God something pleasurable and refreshing to you or do you tend to see it as more of a spiritual discipline that is constraining?

Day 3

READ PSALM 31:14-15

"But as for me, I trust in You, O Lord, I say, 'You are my God.' My times are in Your hand…"

CONSIDER:

Are you cultivating an atmosphere in your life that will naturally produce spiritual vitality? If not, how can you? Will it take trusting God with your time? In what ways, if any, is it more difficult to trust God with your time than it is to trust Him in other areas?

As you've done in previous weeks, use this tool to stay connected with Christ on your own, between your group meetings. This is not "required" but it is an optional tool to keep you thinking about what you discussed in group. Each day, read the verse given. Take your time. You may even want to imagine that Jesus is sitting with you, speaking to you. You may want to use a Bible app to look up commentary or another translation of the verses.

On the first day of the week, you may want to read through all of the verses given for the week so you can get the "big picture" of the passage. After that, walk slowly verse by verse. Listen to what God wants to say to you through His Word, and respond to Him as you meditate on the truths of Scripture.

Day 4

READ PROVERBS 3:1-2

"My son, do not forget my teaching, but let your heart keep my commandments, for length of days and years of life and peace they will add to you."

CONSIDER:

When a lawyer (or Pharisee) asked Jesus "which is the greatest commandment in the Law?" Jesus answered him, "You should love the Lord your God with all your heart, and with all your soul, and with all your mind…[and] you should love your neighbor as yourself." In the above verse from Proverbs, it says to "let your heart keep my commandments." Because of our relationship with Jesus, we are not yoked to the old covenantal law. Jesus has set us free from the law of sin and death (Romans 8:2)! Our new commandments are to love God and love people with everything we have. In what way does making time for wholeness and spiritual vitality in your schedule give you the space and time to love God and others more fully?

Day 5

READ 1 CORINTHIANS 9:24-27

"Do you not know that in a race all the runners run, but only one gets the prize? Run in such a way as to get the prize. Everyone who competes in the games goes into strict training. They do it to get a crown that will not last, but we do it to get a crown that will last forever. Therefore I do not run like someone running aimlessly; I do not fight like a boxer beating the air. No, I strike a blow to my body and make it my slave so that after I have preached to others, I myself will not be disqualified for the prize."

CONSIDER:

Dallas Willard makes this profound statement, "Grace is not opposed to effort; it is opposed to earning." In 1 Corinthians 9:24-27, Paul paints a picture of the effort required in the Christian life through the metaphors of running a race and boxing. It will take effort to be intentional with your time. What practical steps will you take to be more intentional with your time this next week?

Day 6

Use the following space to write any thoughts about what God has been speaking to you through this week's session and during your devotional time. You may also want to write down observations or questions that you'd like to share with the group at your next meeting.

6

SESSION SIX

Personal Wholeness

MEMORY Verse

"Behold, You desire truth in the innermost being, And in the hidden part You will make me know wisdom." (Psalm 51:6 NASB)

Personal Honesty

Have you ever experienced a disconnect between your inner and outer world? For example, saying yes to something that you really don't like or want to do? Or maybe not being totally honest with someone about how you truly feel? The longer we allow the disconnect between the inner and outer world to exist, the wider the gap grows between who we pretend to be and who we truly are.

One of the most courageous things we can ever do is to be truly honest with ourselves. As we open our hearts to the light of God's truth, He will begin to close that gap. His desire, first and foremost, is for us to live with integrity. As Psalm 51 says, "He desires truth in our inner being." Let's begin cultivating a life of personal honesty today by first being honest with ourselves.

SHARE your story

Open your group with prayer. It's week six of your study and it is time to celebrate all that God has done.

Ask everyone to share a little about their experience in the group over the last five weeks. As we have said in previous lessons, sharing our personal stories builds deeper connections among group members. Your story may be exactly what another person needs to hear to encourage or strengthen them. And your listening to others' stories is an act of love and kindness to them—and could very well help them to grow spiritually. Ask your group, "What has surprised you most about this group? Where did God meet you over the last six weeks?"

Begin your time together by using the following icebreaker to get people talking.

Icebreaker:

How would people describe your communication style?

- ☐ Syrupy Sweet
- ☐ Brutally Blunt
- ☐ Politically Correct
- ☐ Other ____________________

WATCH NOW:

DVD SESSION 6

Watch the DVD for this session now. Discuss the teaching you just experienced, as well as the Bible passage below.

DISCUSSION

1. If you think of your public and private worlds like the alignment of a car, how aligned are your public (outer) and private worlds (inner)?

   ☐ A little vibration when I drive
   ☐ Pulling badly
   ☐ Very smooth
   ☐ Other ______________________

2. Why is it so hard to be honest with our ourselves and with others?

3. Agree or disagree and why?
   Being honest with others means you will hurt others' feelings.

4. What do the following verses teach us about being honest?

   "...but speaking the truth in love, we are to grow up in all aspects into Him who is the head, even Christ." Ephesians 4:15 New American Standard Bible (NASB)

   "Therefore, laying aside falsehood, speak truth each one of you with his neighbor, for we are members of one another." Ephesians 4:25 New American Standard Bible (NASB)

5. What do you think of Kerri's one principle for sustaining a life of wholeness: Be completely honest with yourself.

APPLICATION

6. What is one step that you will take this next week to be more honest with yourself and with others? A step may be to keep a honesty journal and notice how you do with being honest in your conversations with others and commitments you make to others.

If your group still needs to make decisions about continuing to meet after this session, have that discussion now. Talk about what you will study, who will lead, and where and when you will meet.

Review your Group Agreement on page 76 and evaluate how well you met your goals. Discuss any changes you want to make as you move forward. If you plan to continue meeting, and your group starts a new study, this is a great time to take on a new role or change roles of service in your group. What new role will you take on? If you are uncertain, maybe your group members have some ideas for you. Remember you aren't making a lifetime commitment to the new role; it will only be for a few weeks. Maybe someone would like to share a role with you if you don't feel ready to serve solo.

Close by praying for prayer requests and take a couple of minutes to review the praises you have recorded over the past five weeks on the Prayer and Praise Report on page 86. Spend some time just worshipping God and thanking Him for all He's done in your group during this study.

notes

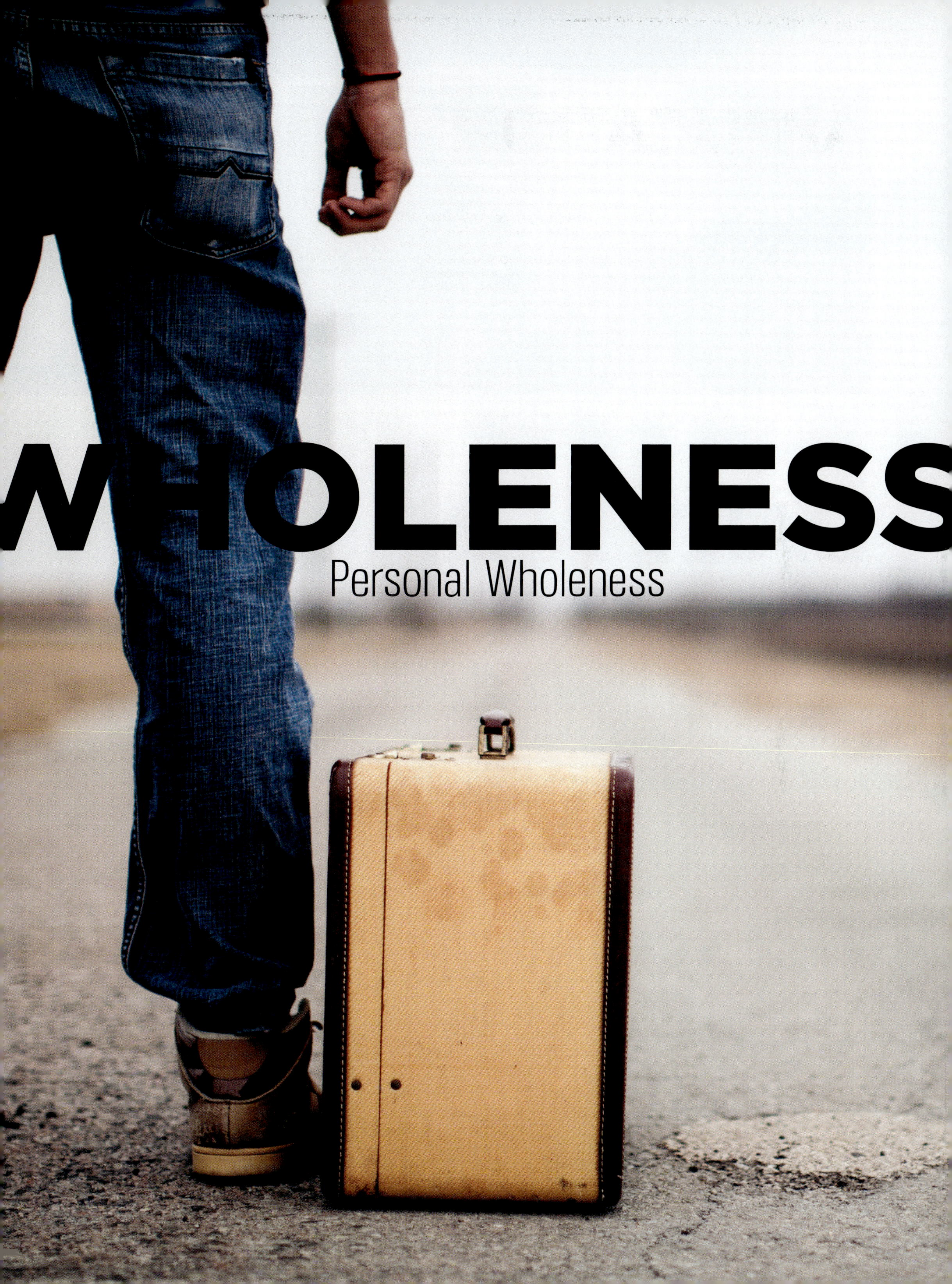

WHOLENESS

Personal Wholeness

DAILY devotions

Day 1

READ JOHN 8:32
"And you will know the truth, and the truth will set you free."

CONSIDER:
What intimidates you the most about being 100% honest with yourself? Are you afraid to really examine your motives? Are you afraid of conflict? How does God's grace help you in these areas?

Day 2

READ PROVERBS 16:13
"Righteous lips are the delight of a King, and He loves him who speaks what is right."

CONSIDER:
How are you using your speech? Are you speaking with integrity? What opportunities do you see for growth in this area?

Day 3

READ LUKE 6:31
"And as you wish that others would do to you, do so to them."

CONSIDER:
How are you using your influence? Are you wielding it responsibly and righteously? Or in manipulation according to what you would like to be done? How do you want people who hold positions of influence in your life to use that influence?

In this last week, begin to pray about your next step in growing closer to Jesus. Use these devotions on your own to stay connected with Him. Now that you're done with the study, you may want to use them as a model for how to reflect and read on your own. Each day, read the verse given. Take your time. Walk slowly verse by verse, listening to Jesus and responding to Him as you meditate on the truths of Scripture and experience His presence.

Study Tip: On the first day of the week, you may want to read through all of the verses given for the week so you can get the "big picture" of the passage. After that, walk slowly verse by verse. Listen to what God wants to say to you through His Word, and respond to Him as you meditate on the truths of Scripture.

Day 4

READ GALATIANS 5:22-23
"But the fruit of the Spirit is love, joy, peace, patience, kindness, goodness, faithfulness, gentleness, self-control; against such things there is no law."

CONSIDER:
One of the fruits of the Spirit is self-control. A part of self-control is setting healthy boundaries in your life. Boundaries are not meant to be an end in themselves, but a means to attain the true goal of wholeness. Healthy boundaries come from a place of wholeness. What are boundaries that you have set in your life?

Day 5

READ ROMANS 14:10
"...each of us will give an account of himself to God."

CONSIDER:
Have you ever taken an honest look at your motives? What are the real reasons you do the things you do...even things you know are not God's best for you? Do you think it is important to understand our own motives? Why or why not?

Day 6

Use the following space to write any thoughts about what God has been speaking to you through this week's session and during your devotional time. You may also want to write down observations or questions that you'd like to share with the group at your next meeting.

FREQUENTYLY asked QUESTIONS

What do we do on the first night of our group?

Like all fun things in life—have a party! A "get to know you" coffee, dinner, or dessert is a great way to launch a new study. It will also help people feel comfortable and welcome. You may want to review the Group Agreement (page 76) and share the names of a few friends you can invite to join. But most importantly, have fun before your study time begins.

Where do we find new members for our group?

This can be troubling, especially for new groups that have only a few people or for existing groups that lose a few people along the way. We encourage you to pray with your group and then brainstorm a list of people from work, church, your neighborhood, your children's school, family, the gym, etc. Then have each group member invite some of the people on his or her list.

No matter how you find members, try to stay on the lookout for new people to join your group. All groups tend to go through healthy attrition–the result of moves, releasing new leaders, ministry opportunities, and so forth–and if the group gets too small, it could be at risk of shutting down. If you and your group stay open, you'll be amazed at the people God sends your way. The next person just might become a friend for life. You never know!

How long will this group meet?

It's totally up to the group. Most groups meet weekly. We strongly recommend that the group meet every week for two six-week sessions. This allows for continuity, and if people miss a meeting they aren't gone for a whole month.

At the end of this study, each group member will decide if he or she wants to continue on for another study. Some groups launch relationships for years to come, and others are stepping-stones into another group experience. Either way, enjoy the journey.

Can we do this study on our own?

Absolutely! This may sound crazy but one of the best ways to do a study is not with a full house but with a few friends. You may choose to gather with one other couple who would enjoy going to the movies or having a quiet dinner and then walking through this study. Jesus will be with you even if there are only two of you (Matthew 18:20).

What if this group is not working for us?

You're not alone! This could be the result of a personality conflict, life stage difference, geographical distance, level of spiritual maturity, or any number of things. Relax. Pray for God's direction, and at the end of this six-week study, decide whether to continue with this group or find another. You don't buy the first car you test drive or marry the first person you date, and the same goes with a group. Don't bail out before the six weeks are up–God might have something to teach you. Also, don't run from conflict or prejudge people before you have given them a chance. God is still working in you too!

Who is the leader?

Most groups have an official leader. But ideally, the group will mature and members will rotate the leadership of meetings. We have discovered that healthy groups rotate hosts/leaders and homes on a regular basis. This model ensures that all members grow, give their unique contribution, and develop their gifts. Christ has promised to be in your midst as you gather, which means that ultimately, God is your leader each step of the way. That should give your group (and whoever may be leading each week) confidence.

How do we handle the child care needs in our group?

Very carefully, as this can be a sensitive issue. We suggest that the group spend some time openly brainstorming solutions. You may try one option that works for a while and then adjust over time. Our favorite approach is for adults to meet in the living room or dining room, and to share the cost of a babysitter (or two) who can be with the kids in a different part of the house. That way, parents don't have to be away from their children all evening when they are too young to be left at home. A second option is to use one home for the kids and a second home (close by or a phone call away) for the adults. A third idea is to rotate the responsibility of providing a lesson or care for the children either in the same home or in another home nearby. This can be an incredible blessing for kids. Finally, the most common idea is to make your own arrangements for child care. No matter what decision the group makes, the best approach is to talk openly about both the problem and the solution.

SMALL group AGREEMENT

OUR PURPOSE:

To talk about what it means to live a God-first life with a few friends.

Group Attendance	To give priority to the group meeting. We will call or email if we will be late or absent. (Completing the Group Calendar on page 78 will minimize this issue.)
Safe Environment	To help create a safe place where people can be heard and feel loved.
Respect Differences	To be gentle and gracious toward people with different spiritual maturity, personal opinions, temperaments, or "imperfections" in fellow group members. We are all works in progress.
Confidentiality	To keep anything that is shared strictly confidential and within the group, and to avoid sharing improper information about those outside the group.
Encouragement for Growth	Accept one another as we are while encouraging one another to grow.
Shared Ownership	To remember that every member is a minister and to ensure that each attender will share a small team role or responsibility over time.
Rotating Hosts/ Leaders and Homes	To encourage different people to host the group in their homes, and to rotate the responsibility of facilitating each meeting. (See the Group Calendar on page 78.)

OUR *time* TOGETHER

Refreshments/mealtimes be provided by:	
The arrangement for childcare will be:	
When we will meet (day of week):	
Where we will meet (place):	
We will begin at (time):	
We will do our best to have some or all of us attend a worship service together. Our primary worship service time will be:	
Date of this agreement:	
Date we will review this agreement again:	

SMALL group CALENDAR

Planning can help ensure the greatest participation at every meeting. At the end of each meeting, review this calendar. Be sure to include a regular rotation of host homes/leaders, and don't forget birthdays, socials, church events, holidays, and mission/ministry projects.

DATE	LESSON	HOST HOME	REFRESHMENTS	LEADER
Monday Jan 15	1	Bill	Joe	Bill

SMALL group ROSTER

	PRAYER requests	PRAISE reports
session 1		
session 2		
session 3		
session 4		
session 5		
session 6		

Session 1
"Come to Me, all you who are weary and burdened, and I will give you rest. Take My yoke upon you and learn from Me, for I am gentle and humble in heart, and you will find rest for your souls. For My yoke is easy and My burden is light."
(Matthew 11:28-30 NIV)

Session 2
"But he was wounded for our transgressions, he was bruised for our iniquities: the chastisement of our peace was upon him; and with his stripes we are healed."
(Isaiah 53:5 KJV)

Session 3
"Then he said to them, 'The Sabbath was made for man, not man for the Sabbath.'"
(Mark 2:27 NIV)

Session 4
"The Word became flesh and blood, and moved into the neighborhood. We saw the glory with our own eyes, the one-of-a-kind glory, like Father, like Son, Generous inside and out, true from start to finish."
(John 1:14 MSG)

MEMORY

Session 5
"Therefore, since we have so great a cloud of witnesses surrounding us, let us also lay aside every encumbrance and the sin which so easily entangles us, and let us run with endurance the race that is set before us."
(Hebrews 12:1 NASB)

Session 6
"Behold, You desire truth in the innermost being, And in the hidden part You will make me know wisdom."
(Psalm 51:6 NASB)

VERSES

HOSTING an OPEN HOUSE

If you're starting a new group, or if this is your first time leading a small group, you should consider planning an "open house" before your first formal group meeting. Even if you only have two to four core members, it's a great way to break the ice and to consider prayerfully who else might be open to join you over the next few weeks. You can also use this kick-off meeting to hand out study guides, spend some time getting to know each other, discuss each person's expectations for the group, and briefly pray for each other.

A simple meal or good desserts always make a kick-off meeting more fun. After people introduce themselves and share how they ended up being at the meeting, have everyone respond to a few icebreaker questions, like: "What is your favorite family vacation?" or "What is one thing you love about your church/ our community?" or "What are three things about your life growing up that most people here don't know?" Finally, ask everyone to tell what he or she hopes to get out of the study. You might want to review the Small Group Agreement and talk about each person's expectations and priorities.

You can skip this kick-off meeting if your time is limited, but an open house can help set your group up for success.

LEADING for the FIRST TIME

Sweaty palms are a healthy sign.

The Bible says God is gracious to the humble. Remember who is in control. Those who are soft in heart (and sweaty palmed) are those whom God is sure to speak through. God wants to use you exactly as you are to lead your group this week.

Seek support.

Ask your co-leader or a close friend to pray for you and prepare with you before the session. Walking through the study will help you anticipate potentially difficult questions and discussion topics.

Prepare.

Prepare. Prepare. Go through the session several times prior to meeting. If you are using the DVD, watch the teaching segment. Consider writing in a journal or fasting for a day to prepare yourself for what God wants to do.

Ask for feedback so you can grow.

Perhaps in an email or on cards handed out at the study, have everyone write down three things you did well and one thing you could improve. Don't get defensive; instead, show an openness to learn and grow.

Share with your group what God is doing in your heart.

God is searching for those whose hearts are fully his. Share your struggles and your victories. People will relate and your willingness to share will encourage them to do the same.

LEADERSHIP TRAINING 101

Thank you! You have responded to the call to help shepherd Jesus' flock. There are few other tasks in the family of God that are as challenging, rewarding, and humbling as this. As you prepare to lead – whether it is one session or the entire series – here are a few thoughts to keep in mind. It might be helpful for you to read these and review them before each session.

1. Remember that you are not alone. God knows everything about you, and he knew that you would be asked to lead your group. God promises, "Never will I leave you; never will I forsake you" (Hebrews 13:5). Whether you are leading for one evening or for the whole study, you will be blessed as you serve. It might be helpful to enlist a co-leader to help you lead the group. This is your chance to involve as many people as you can in building a healthy group. All you have to do is call and ask people to help; you'll be surprised at the response.

2. Just be yourself. Your group needs you to be you! God wants you to use your unique gifts and personality. Don't try to do things exactly like another leader; do them in a way that fits you. Admit it when you don't have an answer, and apologize when you make a mistake. Your group will love you for it, and you'll sleep better at night!

3. Prepare for your meeting ahead of time. Review the session along with the leader's notes, and write down your responses to each question. Be sure you understand how an exercise works, and bring any necessary supplies (such as paper and pens) to your meeting. If the exercise employs one of the items in the appendix, be sure to look over that item so you'll be familiar with it. For encouragement, look up each of the five passages listed below. Read each one as a devotional exercise to help equip yourself with a shepherd's heart. If you do this, you will be more than ready for each meeting.

Matthew 9:36 | 1 Peter 5:2-4 | Psalm 23
Ezekiel 34:11-16 | 1 Thessalonians 2:7-8, 11-12

4. Pray for your group members by name. Before you begin your session, go around the room in your mind and pray for each member by name. You may want to review the prayer list at least once a week. Ask God to use your time together to touch the heart of every person uniquely. Expect God to lead you to whomever He wants you to encourage or challenge in a special way. If you listen, God will surely lead!

5. Learn the rhythm of asking questions. When guiding the discussion, always read aloud the transitional paragraphs and the questions. This will help the group to transition to a time of reflection and response. You can read them yourself, or you can ask for a volunteer, and then be patient until someone begins. Be sure to thank the person who reads aloud.

   When you ask the group a question, be patient. Someone will eventually respond. Sometimes people need a moment or two of silence to think about the question, and if silence doesn't bother you, it won't bother anyone else. After someone responds, thank them and then ask if anyone else would like to share. Be sensitive to new people or reluctant members who aren't ready to say, pray or do anything. If you give them a safe setting, they will open up over time.

6. Be attentive to the needs of the group. If your group has more than seven people, it might be a good idea to gather in discussion circles of three or four people during the DISCUSSION or APPLICATION sections of the study. With a greater opportunity to talk in a small circle, people will connect more with the study. A small circle also encourages a quiet person to participate and tends to minimize the effects of a more vocal or dominant member. Small circles are also helpful during prayer time. People who are unaccustomed to praying aloud will feel more comfortable trying it with just two or three others. When you gather back with the whole group, you can have one person summarize the highlights and prayer requests from each circle.

7. Rotate leaders weekly. At the end of each meeting, ask the group who should lead the following week. Let the group help select your weekly facilitator. You may be perfectly capable of leading each time but you will help others grow in their faith and gifts if you give them opportunities to lead. If you and your group prefer, you can use the Small Group Calendar to fill in the names of all meeting leaders at once.

PRAYER & PRAISE

THE AUTHOR

Kerri Weems

Kerri Weems and her husband, Stovall Weems, are founders of Celebration Church based in Jacksonville, FL. In 1998, Kerri and Stovall moved from Baton Rouge, LA to Jacksonville to plant Celebration with an initial launch team of 7 people. Since then, Celebration has grown to multiple locations regionally throughout Florida, with more than twelve thousand people in weekly attendance. There are additional international locations in Costa Rica, Northern Ireland, and Zimbabwe, Africa.

Kerri serves on the Senior Executive Team at Celebration, leading several ministry areas including staff development, life development, and Celebration Sisterhood. She is passionate about empowering others to live out their fullest potential at every stage of life and sphere of influence. With a certifications in several areas of leadership and organizational development, Kerri especially enjoys coaching ministry leaders and teams in developing their strengths and finding personal wholeness.

In addition to being a gifted writer, teacher, and conference speaker, Kerri is the founder and host of SHINE, Celebration Church's annual women's conference. Every year, the conference reaches thousands of women regionally and globally. Beginning in 2011, SHINE also expanded to Africa for SHINE Zimbabwe.

Kerri is the author of the book *Rhythms of Grace* published through Zondervan, and *Clueless: 10 Things I Wish I Knew About Motherhood Before I Became a Mom.* Kerri and Stovall have three children and live in Jacksonville, Florida.